I dedicate this book to those who see the world in their own unique way—and to Tatai, who taught me that true vision comes from heart.

A Ké-mel creation - bringing stories to life.

Title: Tatai, the little dog who was afraid of the dark.

Copyright © 2025 by Chris Kemel

Ilustrations copyright Chris Kemel

All rights reseved. No part of this book may be reproduced in any form without written permisson from publisher.

1st edition

ISBN: 978-1-0693722-4-6

Ké-mel publishing
8 Widmer St, 3303 unit
Toronto, Canadá
ON M5V 0W6

English language

Once upon a time, there was a very adorable little dog named Tatai.

He was all white and very fluffy, but he had a tremendous fear of the dark.

Every time Tatai thought about exploring more of the house and suddenly came across the dark, he would stop immediately...

... and imagine the "monster of the dark" with big and scary eyes...

... saying:
- "You can't come in here!"
(The monster of the dark would say)
Tatai would shake with fear...

... and run back to his owners or to places with light, where he felt safe.

His owners, Chris, Saaye, and Dada noticed that Tatai would always wait for them to turn on the lights.

With patience and love, his owners used…

... **words of encouragement, playful games,**

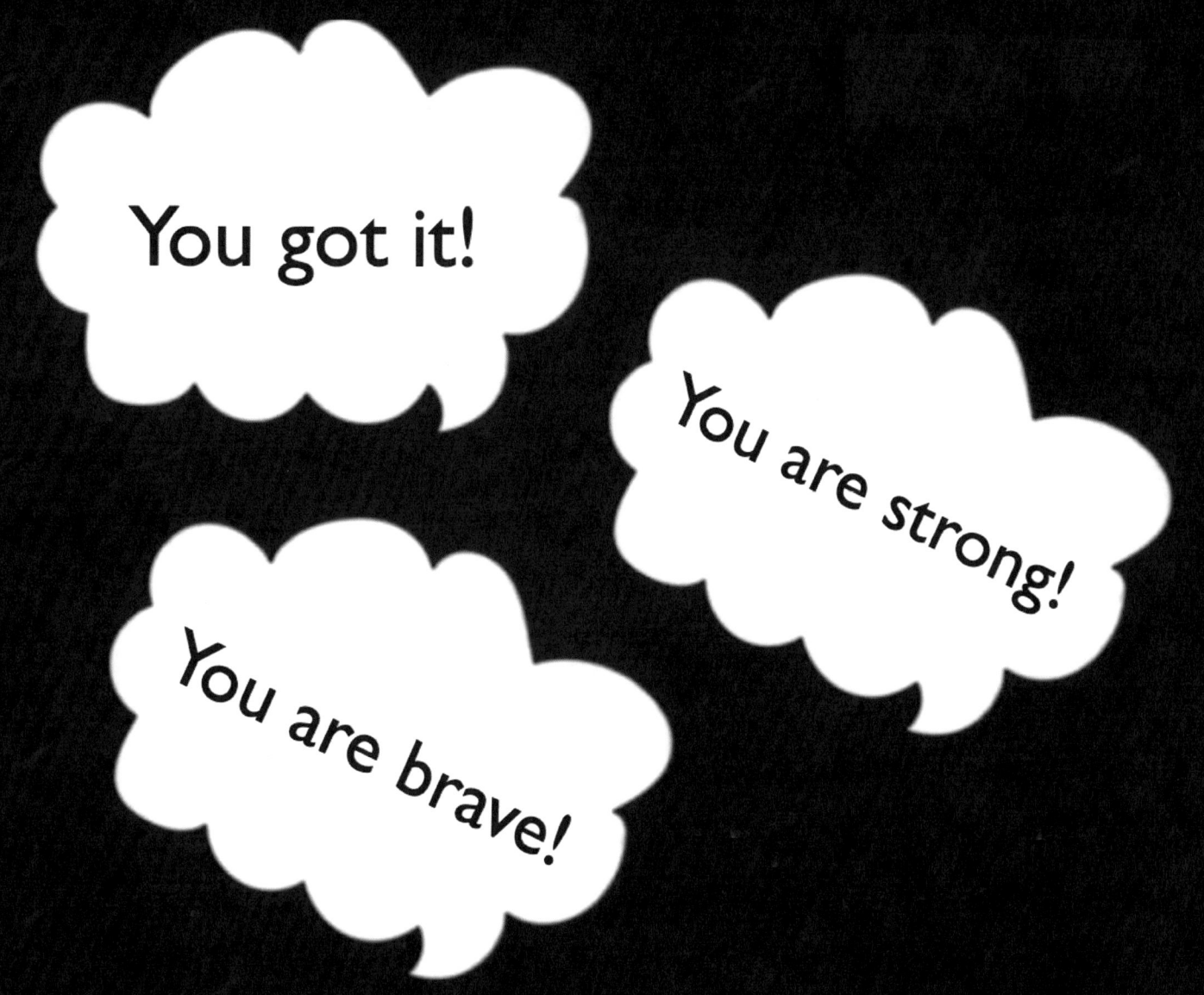

and a special lantern to help him.

One night, Tatai saw his special lantern near the dark hallway. He decided to be brave, just like his owners had encouraged him to be. And there he went, walking through the dark until he reached the light again.

Along the way, the monster of the dark said:

- "How dare you pass through here?"

- "Woof woof!" (Tatai grumbled with a angry face)

Over time, Tatai discovered that the dark wasn't so scary after all.
The monster of the dark kept saying:
- "You can't come in here."

Until Tatai finally said:
- "Woof woof woof!" (Tatai replied)
"I'm not afraid of you anymore!"

Tatai had finally overcome his fear of the dark and realized there were no monsters—just places waiting to be explored.

Chris, Saaye, and Dada also learned something important: When you treat your pets with love, patience, and care, they can overcome any challenge!

Tatai was now a confident and happy little dog, and he knew that his owners loved him unconditionally.

That is the real magic: love changes everything.

Notes:

About the author and Tatai:

Chris Kemel discovered her love for art at an early age and has been passionate about it ever since. With a natural talent for creativity, she has always expressed herself through various artistic forms. She studied at the Pontifical Catholic University of Rio Grande do Sul (PUCRS) in Brazil, where she graduated in Law and discovered her passion for writing. The love for both art and writing came together, and since then, they have walked side by side on her journey. Through her creations, she hopes to inspire, entertain, and bring to life the stories in her mind.

Since 2023, Chris Kemel has also become a language teacher for those who would like to learn Portuguese, Spanish, and English. Her passion for languages and her desire to share knowledge have brought her closer to people from different backgrounds, enriching her journey even further.

This book was inspired by a real Maltese dog. His name is Tiger, and his nickname is Tatai. The love his owner, Chris Kemel, has for him motivated her to write and create inspiring stories for children. Tatai is 12 years old. He was born on the eighth of October, 2012. He is a small, fluffy, white, and cute Brazilian dog with a calm and gentle energy. He loves his family deeply and shows it every day with his warm affection. He always follows them around the house, staying close, just to be near the ones he loves. Despite being calm, Tatai has a playful side that shines through when it's time to play with other dogs or with us. He loves snuggling up and offering his little paw when he wants attention. He's a little angel in disguise, always there when you need him.

One of Tatai's most special traits is that he is always smiling. His cheerful expression makes everyone around him feel warm and loved, as if he's bringing happiness just by being there.

He's the kind of dog that doesn't ask for much, but he gives everything—loyalty, his heart, and his soft, fluffy presence. His love is pure, simple, and constant. No matter what, he'll always be there, making the world just a little bit brighter for the ones he cares about.

Property of:

_____

_____

About the author and Tatai:

Chris Kemel discovered her love for art at an early age and has been passionate about it ever since. With a natural talent for creativity, she has always expressed herself through various artistic forms. She studied at the Pontifical Catholic University of Rio Grande do Sul (PUCRS) in Brazil, where she graduated in Law and discovered her passion for writing. The love for both art and writing came together, and since then, they have walked side by side on her journey. Through her creations, she hopes to inspire, entertain, and bring to life the stories in her mind.

Since 2023, Chris Kemel has also become a language teacher for those who would like to learn Portuguese, Spanish, and English. Her passion for languages and her desire to share knowledge have brought her closer to people from different backgrounds, enriching her journey even further.

This book was inspired by a real Maltese dog. His name is Tiger, and his nickname is Tatai. The love his owner, Chris Kemel, has for him motivated her to write and create inspiring stories for children. Tatai is 12 years old. He was born on the eighth of October, 2012. He is a small, fluffy, white, and cute Brazilian dog with a calm and gentle energy. He loves his family deeply and shows it every day with his warm affection. He always follows them around the house, staying close, just to be near the ones he loves. Despite being calm, Tatai has a playful side that shines through when it's time to play with other dogs or with us. He loves snuggling up and offering his little paw when he wants attention. He's a little angel in disguise, always there when you need him.

One of Tatai's most special traits is that he is always smiling. His cheerful expression makes everyone around him feel warm and loved, as if he's bringing happiness just by being there.

He's the kind of dog that doesn't ask for much, but he gives everything—loyalty, his heart, and his soft, fluffy presence. His love is pure, simple, and constant. No matter what, he'll always be there, making the world just a little bit brighter for the ones he cares about.

Property of:

www.ingramcontent.com/pod-product-compliance
Lightning Source LLC
LaVergne TN
LVRC080917061225
827181LV00014B/49